ABOUT THIS BOOK

Our Gran is one of the senior members of our family.
She has a huge experience about life. She has a huge adventure
in her life which is unknown to us. Sometimes we want to know
about her. But we don't find where to start, what type of
questions we should ask. Sometimes we don't get enough time
to hear her story. But we should save her memory.
So, Through this book we tried to capture her whole life.
There will be **101 questions** including her **Birthday**,
Family, **Growing up**, **Teenage years**, **School**, **Career**,
Relationships, **Friendships**, and **some
Random questions about her whole life**. There will be
enough space to answer each question. At the last of this book,
there will be **10+ free pages where you can include your
own questions**. Through this book, you can know about her
thoughts, what she likes, what she doesn't like, her life
experience and even you can take advice from her.
**I think this book is going to be a great gift for your
Gran.**

CONTENT

IT'S YOUR BIRTHDAY!

1. What is your birthdate? _____

    _____

    _____

    _____

2. What was your full name at birth? Who named you? _____

    _____

    _____

    _____

    _____

3. Were you born in a hospital? If not, where? _____

    _____

    _____

    _____

    _____

4. In which city were you born?_____

    _____

    _____

    _____

IT'S YOUR BIRTHDAY!

5. How old were your parents when you were born?_____

_____

_____

_____

_____

_____

6. Did you do anything funny when you were born?_____

_____

_____

_____

_____

_____

_____

_____

_____

_____

_____

TELL ME ABOUT YOUR FAMILY

1. What were your parent's names? _____

_____

_____

_____

_____

_____

2. What were your parent's professions? _____

_____

_____

_____

_____

_____

_____

_____

_____

_____

_____

_____

_____

3

TELL ME ABOUT YOUR FAMILY

3. What were your parents like? ————————————

_____

_____

_____

_____

_____

_____

_____

_____

_____

_____

_____

_____

_____

_____

_____

_____

_____

_____

TELL ME ABOUT YOUR FAMILY

4. How many siblings do you have? Were you the oldest, middle, or youngest in position? Describe the personalities of each of your siblings- _____

_____

_____

_____

_____

_____

_____

_____

_____

_____

_____

_____

_____

_____

_____

_____

_____

5

TELL ME ABOUT YOUR FAMILY

5. How did your family spend the holidays? _____

_____

_____

_____

_____

_____

_____

_____

_____

_____

_____

_____

_____

_____

_____

_____

_____

_____

_____

TELL ME ABOUT YOUR FAMILY

6. How did your family spend time together when you were young?

_____

_____

_____

_____

_____

_____

_____

_____

_____

_____

_____

_____

_____

_____

_____

_____

_____

_____

TELL ME ABOUT YOUR FAMILY

7. Were you an obedient or misbehaving child? ——————

_____

_____

_____

_____

_____

_____

8. What was the special meal your mother made for you? ——

_____

_____

_____

_____

_____

_____

_____

_____

_____

_____

_____

TELL ME ABOUT YOUR FAMILY

9. What is a special memory you have of your mother? _____

_____

_____

_____

_____

_____

_____

_____

_____

_____

_____

_____

_____

_____

_____

_____

_____

_____

TELL ME ABOUT YOUR FAMILY

10. What do you remember about your grandparents? Did they ever make you laugh? _____

_____

_____

_____

_____

_____

_____

_____

_____

_____

_____

_____

_____

_____

_____

_____

_____

TELL ME ABOUT YOUR FAMILY

11. Are there any funny or unusual things you remember your children doing? _____

_____

_____

_____

_____

_____

_____

_____

_____

_____

_____

_____

_____

_____

_____

_____

_____

GROWING UP

1. Where did you grow up? What was it like there? _____

_____

_____

_____

_____

_____

_____

_____

_____

_____

_____

_____

_____

_____

_____

_____

_____

_____

GROWING UP

2. Who was your childhood best friend? What specialty did he/she have? _____

_____

_____

_____

_____

_____

_____

3. Who was your childhood favorite person? What specialty did he/she have? _____

_____

_____

_____

_____

_____

_____

_____

13

GROWING UP

4. Have you ever done anything crazy? What was it? _____

_____

_____

_____

_____

_____

_____

_____

_____

_____

_____

_____

_____

_____

_____

_____

_____

_____

GROWING UP

5. What did your childhood bedroom look like? _____

_____

_____

_____

_____

_____

_____

_____

_____

_____

_____

_____

_____

_____

_____

_____

_____

_____

GROWING UP

6. What was your bedtime as a child? _____

_____

_____

_____

_____

7. What were your fondest memories as a child? _____

_____

_____

_____

_____

_____

_____

_____

_____

_____

_____

_____

_____

_____

GROWING UP

8. What was your favorite television show as a child? _____

_____

_____

_____

_____

_____

_____

_____

_____

_____

_____

_____

_____

_____

_____

GROWING UP

9. What kinds of games did you play? _____

_____

_____

_____

_____

_____

_____

_____

_____

_____

_____

_____

_____

_____

_____

_____

_____

_____

GROWING UP

10. What did you want to be when you grew up? Why?

GROWING UP

11. What challenges did you have growing up? ─────────

_____

_____

_____

_____

_____

_____

_____

_____

_____

_____

_____

_____

_____

_____

_____

_____

GROWING UP

12. Did you ever go on vacation as a child? Where did you go?

If yes, tell me about it- _____

_____

_____

_____

_____

_____

_____

_____

_____

_____

_____

_____

_____

_____

_____

_____

_____

_____

GROWING UP

THE TEENAGE YEARS

1. Who was your teenage best friend? What specialty did he/she have? _____

_____

_____

_____

_____

_____

_____

_____

_____

_____

_____

_____

_____

_____

_____

_____

_____

THE TEENAGE YEARS

2. Did you ever have a pet? What was it? What was the name of your pet? _____

_____

_____

_____

_____

_____

_____

3. Did you ever break curfew or sneak out of the house? If yes, tell me the story.. _____

_____

_____

_____

_____

_____

_____

_____

_____

_____

THE TEENAGE YEARS

_____

_____

_____

_____

_____

_____

_____

_____

_____

_____

_____

_____

_____

_____

_____

_____

_____

_____

_____

THE TEENAGE YEARS

4. Did you get an allowance? How much was it? and How did you spend your money? _____

_____

_____

_____

_____

_____

_____

_____

_____

_____

_____

_____

_____

_____

_____

_____

THE TEENAGE YEARS

5. What was dating like when you were a teenager? _____

_____

_____

_____

_____

_____

_____

_____

_____

_____

_____

_____

_____

_____

_____

THE TEENAGE YEARS

6. Who was your celebrity crush? _____

_____

_____

_____

_____

7. Who was your favorite writer? _____

_____

_____

_____

_____

8. What did you do to celebrate birthdays? _____

_____

_____

_____

_____

_____

_____

_____

_____

THE TEENAGE YEARS

29

THE TEENAGE YEARS

9. What activities did you enjoy in your free time? ──────

_____

_____

_____

_____

_____

_____

_____

_____

_____

_____

_____

_____

_____

_____

_____

_____

_____

THE TEENAGE YEARS

10. What do you remember most about your teenage years?
    Tell me about it- _____

_____

_____

_____

_____

_____

_____

_____

_____

_____

_____

_____

_____

_____

_____

_____

THE TEENAGE YEARS

11. How would people describe you who knew your teenage years?

_____

_____

_____

_____

_____

_____

_____

_____

_____

_____

_____

_____

12. Describe your teenage self in 3 words. _____

_____

_____

_____

_____

SCHOOL

1. What was your school name? _____

_____

_____

_____

_____

2. What were the most popular clothes in school? _____

_____

_____

_____

_____

_____

_____

_____

_____

_____

_____

_____

_____

SCHOOL

3. Who was your favorite teacher? Why? ⎯⎯⎯⎯⎯

⎯⎯⎯⎯⎯⎯⎯⎯⎯⎯⎯⎯⎯⎯⎯⎯⎯⎯⎯⎯⎯⎯⎯⎯

⎯⎯⎯⎯⎯⎯⎯⎯⎯⎯⎯⎯⎯⎯⎯⎯⎯⎯⎯⎯⎯⎯⎯⎯

⎯⎯⎯⎯⎯⎯⎯⎯⎯⎯⎯⎯⎯⎯⎯⎯⎯⎯⎯⎯⎯⎯⎯⎯

⎯⎯⎯⎯⎯⎯⎯⎯⎯⎯⎯⎯⎯⎯⎯⎯⎯⎯⎯⎯⎯⎯⎯⎯

⎯⎯⎯⎯⎯⎯⎯⎯⎯⎯⎯⎯⎯⎯⎯⎯⎯⎯⎯⎯⎯⎯⎯⎯

⎯⎯⎯⎯⎯⎯⎯⎯⎯⎯⎯⎯⎯⎯⎯⎯⎯⎯⎯⎯⎯⎯⎯⎯

⎯⎯⎯⎯⎯⎯⎯⎯⎯⎯⎯⎯⎯⎯⎯⎯⎯⎯⎯⎯⎯⎯⎯⎯

⎯⎯⎯⎯⎯⎯⎯⎯⎯⎯⎯⎯⎯⎯⎯⎯⎯⎯⎯⎯⎯⎯⎯⎯

⎯⎯⎯⎯⎯⎯⎯⎯⎯⎯⎯⎯⎯⎯⎯⎯⎯⎯⎯⎯⎯⎯⎯⎯

⎯⎯⎯⎯⎯⎯⎯⎯⎯⎯⎯⎯⎯⎯⎯⎯⎯⎯⎯⎯⎯⎯⎯⎯

⎯⎯⎯⎯⎯⎯⎯⎯⎯⎯⎯⎯⎯⎯⎯⎯⎯⎯⎯⎯⎯⎯⎯⎯

⎯⎯⎯⎯⎯⎯⎯⎯⎯⎯⎯⎯⎯⎯⎯⎯⎯⎯⎯⎯⎯⎯⎯⎯

⎯⎯⎯⎯⎯⎯⎯⎯⎯⎯⎯⎯⎯⎯⎯⎯⎯⎯⎯⎯⎯⎯⎯⎯

⎯⎯⎯⎯⎯⎯⎯⎯⎯⎯⎯⎯⎯⎯⎯⎯⎯⎯⎯⎯⎯⎯⎯⎯

⎯⎯⎯⎯⎯⎯⎯⎯⎯⎯⎯⎯⎯⎯⎯⎯⎯⎯⎯⎯⎯⎯⎯⎯

⎯⎯⎯⎯⎯⎯⎯⎯⎯⎯⎯⎯⎯⎯⎯⎯⎯⎯⎯⎯⎯⎯⎯⎯

SCHOOL

4. Who were some of your friends at school? Tell me about them-

---

SCHOOL

SCHOOL

5. What were you like during school? (Class, clown, shy, etc)

_____

_____

_____

_____

_____

_____

_____

6. What were you good at in school? Did you have a favorite
   subject? _____

_____

_____

_____

_____

_____

_____

_____

_____

SCHOOL

7. Did you study for exams long before they happened or cram the night before? Tell me about your study plan. _____

_____

_____

_____

_____

_____

_____

_____

_____

_____

_____

_____

_____

_____

_____

_____

SCHOOL

8. What were the most popular toys or gadgets? _____

_____

_____

_____

_____

_____

_____

_____

9. Did you (play /want to play) any specific musical instrument?

_____

_____

_____

_____

_____

_____

_____

_____

_____

SCHOOL

10. What sports/games did you like to play? Tell me about it. ____

_____

_____

_____

_____

_____

_____

_____

_____

_____

_____

_____

_____

_____

_____

_____

_____

SCHOOL

11. Did you participate in any other extracurricular activities like theater, debate, church youth group, etc? _____

_____

_____

_____

_____

_____

_____

_____

12. What were some of the fashions when you were in high school?

_____

_____

_____

_____

_____

_____

_____

_____

_____

41

CAREER

1. How many jobs have you had? _____

   _____

   _____

   _____

   _____

   _____

2. What was your first job? And how much money had you
   generated? _____

   _____

   _____

   _____

   _____

   _____

   _____

   _____

   _____

   _____

   _____

CAREER

3. Which one was your favorite job and why? _____

_____

_____

_____

_____

_____

_____

_____

_____

_____

_____

_____

_____

_____

_____

_____

_____

_____

CAREER

4. What was one of the hardest parts of being in the workforce? Why? _____

_____

_____

_____

_____

_____

_____

_____

_____

_____

_____

_____

_____

_____

_____

_____

CAREER

5. Did you get any mentors? Who was one of your biggest mentors? Tell me about it. _____

_____

_____

_____

_____

_____

_____

_____

_____

_____

_____

_____

_____

_____

_____

_____

_____

CAREER

6. When did you open your first bank account? _____

_____

_____

_____

7. In your opinion, which profession is best and why? _____

_____

_____

_____

_____

_____

_____

_____

_____

_____

_____

_____

_____

CAREER

8. Do you have any job advice for me when I start working? ___

_____

_____

_____

_____

_____

_____

_____

_____

_____

_____

_____

_____

_____

_____

_____

_____

_____

CAREER

_____

_____

_____

_____

_____

_____

_____

_____

_____

_____

_____

_____

_____

_____

_____

_____

_____

ROMANTIC RELATIONSHIPS

1. How did you meet your spouse? What year was it? _____

_____

_____

_____

_____

_____

_____

_____

_____

_____

_____

_____

_____

_____

_____

_____

_____

ROMANTIC RELATIONSHIPS

2. What qualities do you remember liking about them? ———

_____

_____

_____

_____

_____

_____

_____

_____

_____

_____

_____

_____

_____

_____

_____

_____

ROMANTIC RELATIONSHIPS

3. What was your first date? Describe it- _____

_____

_____

_____

_____

_____

_____

_____

_____

_____

_____

_____

_____

_____

_____

_____

_____

_____

_____

ROMANTIC RELATIONSHIPS

4. How did you/he propose? _____

_____

_____

_____

_____

_____

_____

_____

_____

_____

_____

_____

_____

_____

_____

_____

ROMANTIC RELATIONSHIPS

5. When and where did you get married? _____

_____

_____

_____

_____

6. What was one of your favorite parts of marriage? _____

_____

_____

_____

_____

_____

_____

_____

_____

_____

_____

_____

_____

_____

53

ROMANTIC RELATIONSHIPS

7. What was one of the biggest struggles you've overcome together?

_____

_____

_____

_____

_____

_____

_____

_____

_____

_____

_____

_____

_____

_____

_____

_____

ROMANTIC RELATIONSHIPS

8. Do you believe in love at first sight? _____

_____

_____

_____

_____

_____

_____

9. In your opinion, which age is perfect to marry? _____

_____

_____

_____

_____

_____

_____

_____

_____

_____

_____

FRIENDSHIPS

1. How did you meet your best friend growing up? _____

_____

_____

_____

_____

_____

_____

_____

_____

_____

_____

_____

_____

_____

_____

_____

_____

_____

_____

FRIENDSHIPS

2. What did you and your best friend love to do together? _____

_____

_____

_____

_____

_____

_____

_____

_____

_____

_____

_____

_____

_____

_____

_____

_____

_____

FRIENDSHIPS

3. Was there a certain place you and your friends liked to hang out? How was it? _____

_____

_____

_____

_____

_____

_____

_____

_____

_____

_____

_____

_____

_____

_____

_____

FRIENDSHIPS

4. How did you make friends as an adult? What did you like to do together? _____

_____

_____

_____

_____

_____

_____

_____

_____

_____

_____

_____

_____

_____

_____

_____

_____

_____

FRIENDSHIPS

5. What's one of your favorite memories with a friend? _____

_____

_____

_____

_____

_____

_____

_____

_____

_____

_____

_____

_____

_____

_____

_____

_____

_____

FRIENDSHIPS

6. Who is your current best friend? Tell me about him/her- ____

_____

_____

_____

_____

_____

_____

_____

_____

_____

_____

_____

_____

_____

_____

_____

_____

_____

FRIENDSHIPS

7. How do you explain the word "friendship"? _____

_____

_____

_____

_____

_____

_____

_____

_____

_____

_____

_____

_____

_____

_____

_____

_____

ABOUT YOUR WHOLE LIFE

1. Who has made the biggest impact on your life and how? ____

_____

_____

_____

_____

_____

_____

_____

_____

_____

_____

_____

_____

_____

_____

_____

_____

_____

ABOUT YOUR WHOLE LIFE

2. What was the most embarrassing thing that happened to you?

_____

_____

_____

_____

_____

_____

_____

_____

_____

_____

_____

_____

_____

_____

_____

_____

_____

ABOUT YOUR WHOLE LIFE

3. Do you practice a religion? What impact has religion had on your life? _____

_____

_____

_____

_____

_____

_____

_____

_____

_____

_____

_____

_____

_____

_____

_____

_____

ABOUT YOUR WHOLE LIFE

4. What have you always been good at? _____

_____

_____

_____

_____

_____

_____

_____

_____

_____

_____

_____

_____

_____

ABOUT YOUR WHOLE LIFE

5. Who is someone you miss? Why? _____

_____

_____

_____

_____

_____

_____

_____

_____

_____

_____

_____

_____

_____

_____

_____

_____

ABOUT YOUR WHOLE LIFE

6. What is the best decision you have ever made? Why do you
    think it is best? _____

    _____

    _____

    _____

    _____

    _____

    _____

    _____

    _____

    _____

    _____

    _____

    _____

    _____

    _____

    _____

ABOUT YOUR WHOLE LIFE

7. How do you handle stress? Tell me- _____

_____

_____

_____

_____

_____

_____

_____

_____

_____

_____

_____

_____

_____

_____

_____

_____

_____

_____

ABOUT YOUR WHOLE LIFE

8. Do you have any regrets in life? What is it? _____

_____

_____

_____

_____

_____

_____

_____

_____

_____

_____

_____

_____

_____

_____

_____

_____

_____

ABOUT YOUR WHOLE LIFE

9. Tell me about one of your happiest memories- _____

_____

_____

_____

_____

_____

_____

_____

_____

_____

_____

_____

_____

_____

_____

_____

_____

ABOUT YOUR WHOLE LIFE

10. What makes you happy? Tell me- _____

_____

_____

_____

_____

_____

_____

_____

_____

_____

_____

_____

_____

_____

_____

_____

_____

_____

ABOUT YOUR WHOLE LIFE

11. Tell me about when I was born- _____

_____

_____

_____

_____

_____

_____

_____

_____

_____

_____

_____

_____

_____

_____

_____

_____

_____

ABOUT YOUR WHOLE LIFE

12. What is the most important lesson that your parents taught you?

_____

_____

_____

_____

_____

_____

_____

_____

_____

_____

_____

_____

_____

_____

_____

_____

ABOUT YOUR WHOLE LIFE

13. What was the hardest thing for you to go through? Why? ____

_____

_____

_____

_____

_____

_____

_____

_____

_____

_____

_____

_____

_____

_____

_____

_____

_____

ABOUT YOUR WHOLE LIFE

14. If you could go back in time and choose a new career for
yourself, would you? What would you choose? Why? _____

_____

_____

_____

_____

_____

_____

_____

_____

_____

_____

_____

_____

_____

_____

_____

_____

_____

ABOUT YOUR WHOLE LIFE

15. Do you have a favorite age/stage in life? Why? _____

_____

_____

_____

_____

_____

_____

_____

_____

_____

_____

_____

_____

_____

_____

_____

_____

_____

_____

ABOUT YOUR WHOLE LIFE

16. Do you think money can buy happiness? Why or why not? __

_____

_____

_____

_____

_____

_____

_____

_____

_____

_____

_____

_____

_____

_____

_____

ABOUT YOUR WHOLE LIFE

17. What is one thing you want people to remember about you?

_____

_____

_____

_____

_____

_____

_____

_____

_____

_____

_____

_____

_____

_____

_____

_____

79

ABOUT YOUR WHOLE LIFE

18. Which one is your favorite city in the world? Why? _____

_____

_____

_____

_____

_____

_____

_____

_____

_____

_____

_____

_____

_____

_____

_____

_____

ABOUT YOUR WHOLE LIFE

19. Which thing do you like to do? _____

_____

_____

_____

_____

_____

_____

_____

_____

_____

_____

_____

_____

_____

_____

_____

_____

_____

ABOUT YOUR WHOLE LIFE

20. Are there any secrets to living a long, fulfilling life? _____

_____

_____

_____

_____

_____

_____

_____

_____

_____

_____

_____

_____

_____

_____

_____

_____

ABOUT YOUR WHOLE LIFE

21. When you heard you were going to be a mother for the first time, how did you feel? Tell me one of your favorite memories of being a mom- _____

_____

_____

_____

_____

_____

_____

_____

_____

_____

_____

_____

_____

_____

_____

_____

ABOUT YOUR WHOLE LIFE

_____

_____

_____

_____

_____

_____

_____

_____

_____

_____

_____

_____

_____

_____

_____

_____

_____

ABOUT YOUR WHOLE LIFE

22. When you heard you were going to be a grandma for the first time, how did you feel? How old were you when I was born?

_____

_____

_____

_____

_____

_____

_____

_____

_____

_____

_____

_____

_____

_____

ABOUT YOUR WHOLE LIFE

23. What's the most important lesson you have learned during
your life? _____

_____

_____

_____

_____

_____

_____

_____

_____

_____

_____

_____

_____

_____

_____

ABOUT YOUR WHOLE LIFE

24. If there's any piece of advice that you feel you need to share, what would it be? _____

_____

_____

_____

_____

_____

_____

_____

_____

_____

_____

_____

_____

_____

_____

_____

_____

_____

_____

EXTRA PAGE

_____

_____

_____

_____

_____

_____

_____

_____

_____

_____

_____

_____

_____

_____

_____

_____

_____

_____

_____

_____

EXTRA PAGE

EXTRA PAGE

EXTRA PAGE

EXTRA PAGE

EXTRA PAGE

EXTRA PAGE

_____

_____

_____

_____

_____

_____

_____

_____

_____

_____

_____

_____

_____

_____

_____

_____

_____

EXTRA PAGE

EXTRA PAGE

EXTRA PAGE

EXTRA PAGE

EXTRA PAGE

_____

_____

_____

_____

_____

_____

_____

_____

_____

_____

_____

_____

_____

_____

_____

_____

_____

_____

_____

EXTRA PAGE

Made in the USA
Monee, IL
03 May 2022

95794194R00059